SINGING NUMBERS

CD

IMP

International MUSIC Publications

©**International Music Publications Limited**
Griffin House 161 Hammersmith Road London W6 8BS England

Published 2001

Editor: Louisa Wallace
Music Engraving & CD Production: Artemis Music Ltd.
Vocals on Recording: Helen Speirs
Cover Design: Dominic Brookman

Counting Song

Demonstration   Backing

Words and Music by
Eileen Diamond

Brightly

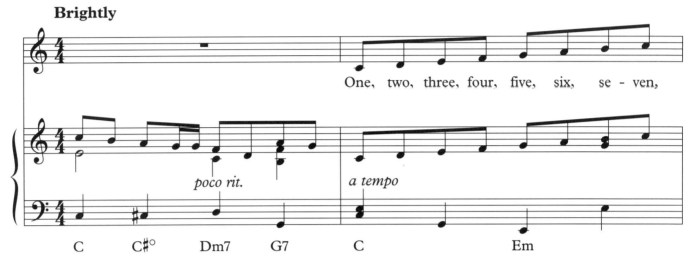

One, two, three, four, five, six, se - ven,

poco rit.   *a tempo*

C   C#°   Dm7   G7   C   Em

eight, nine, ten.   You can count right up to ten and

F   F#°   C   G7   C   Em   D#°

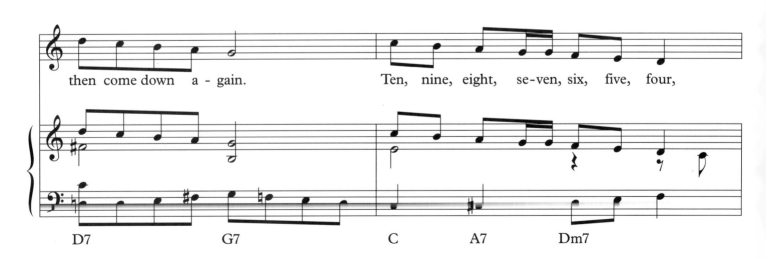

then come down a - gain.   Ten, nine, eight, se - ven, six, five, four,

D7   G7   C   A7   Dm7

© 2001 International Music Publications Ltd, London W6 8BS

three, two, one.　　For-wards　and back-wards,　count-ing can be fun!

G7　G$^+$　C　G7　　C　　　　F　　Dm7　G7　C

One, two, three, four, five, six, seven,
Eight, nine, ten.
You can count right up to ten and then come down again.
Ten, nine, eight, seven, six, five, four,
Three, two, one.
Forwards and backwards,
Counting can be fun!

- A simple counting song to give familiarity with numbers.

4

Demonstration

Backing

Un, Deux, Trois, Quatre

Words and Music by
Eileen Diamond

Steadily

We've learnt to count in

G   Am   D7   G

Eng-lish, it's ea-sy with a song. So if you want to count in French,

Am   D7   G   Am7

Lively, with enthusiasm

(Teacher)   *(Children)*   *(T)*

come and sing a - long.   Un, deux, trois, quatre.   Un, deux, trois, quatre.   Cinq, six, sept.

poco rit.   *a tempo*

A7   D7   G   A7

(Ch)   *(T)*   *(Ch)*   *(T)*

Cinq, six, sept.   Huit, neuf, dix.   Huit, neuf, dix.   All to-ge-ther, tous en *cho-eur.

D7   G   G7

* CHŒUR pronounced KŒR

© 2001 International Music Publications Ltd, London W6 8BS

We've learnt to count in English,
It's easy with a song.
So if you want to count in French,
Come and sing along.

(Teacher): Un, deux, trois, quatre.
(Children): Un, deux, trois, quatre.
(T): Cinq, six, sept.
(Ch): Cinq, six, sept.
(T): Huit, neuf, dix.
(Ch): Huit, neuf, dix.
(T): All together,
Tous en chœur.★
(ALL): One, two three, four, five, six, seven,
Eight, nine, ten.
Un, deux, trois, quatre, cinq, six, sept,
Huit, neuf, dix.
1st time only – (T): Encore!

★ CHŒUR pronounced KŒR.

• It's fun and easy learning French with a song!

6

Clapping Song

Demonstration

Backing

Words and Music by
Eileen Diamond

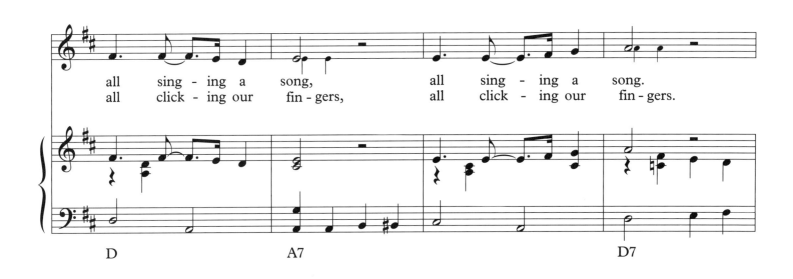

© 2001 International Music Publications Ltd, London W6 8BS

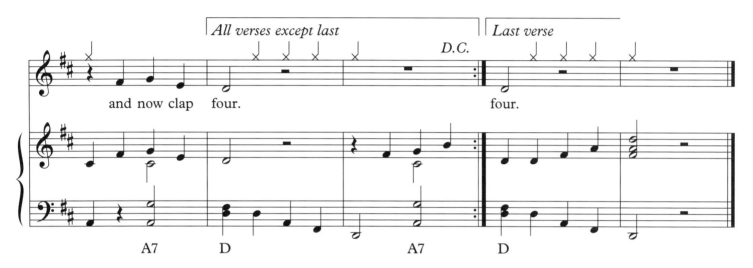

1. We're all singing a song,
   All singing a song.
   La, la, la, la,
   We're all singing a song.

CHORUS: Now clap one, then clap two.
         Then clap three and now clap four.

2. We're all clicking our fingers,
   All clicking our fingers.
   Click, click, click, click,
   We're all clicking our fingers.

   (CHORUS)

3. We're all stretching our arms . . .

   (CHORUS)

4. We're all tapping our feet . . .

- Any activity may be used for the verses. Ask the children for further suggestions.
- In verses 3 & 4 of the recording, percussion has been added just as a fun sound effect.
- *DEVELOPMENT:* Once the song is known, the number of claps in the chorus
                  may be changed at random by the teacher. The children will
                  need to concentrate in order to clap the correct number!

Only One Me

Demonstration   Backing

Words and Music by
Eileen Diamond

laugh and speak, I ans-wer to my name. Yet I'm diff-erent,

F   F#°   Gm   C7   F   A7

I'm u - nique. No - bo-dy's quite the same! 4. There are

Dm   G7   C6   C7

rit.

*___ ___ tea-chers in my school. *___ ___ chil-dren in my

a tempo

F   F#°   Gm   Gm7

class. Lots of peo - ple in my fa - mi - ly,

C7   B♭9   B♭m

but there's on - ly one me. Yes, there's on - ly one me!

F   C7   F#°   D7   Gm   C7+5   F

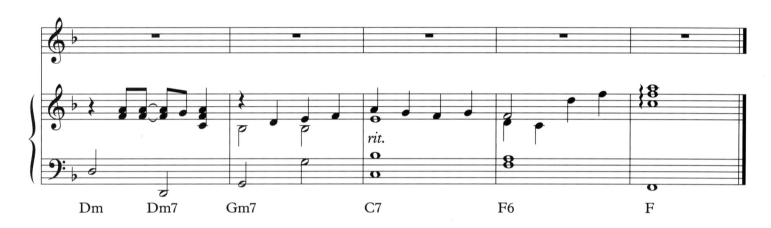

Dm   Dm7   Gm7   C7   F6   F

1. There are millions of people in the world,
   Hundreds of people in the street,
   Lots of people in my family,
   But there's only one me.

2. There are thousands of creatures in the sea,
   Scores of birds up in the sky,
   Lots of people in my family,
   But there's only one me.

3. Like everyone else I laugh and speak,
   I answer to my name.
   Yet I'm different, I'm unique.
   Nobody's quite the same!

4. There are *.. teachers in my school.
   *.. children in my class.
   Lots of people in my family,
   But there's only one me.
   Yes, there's only one me!

---

*.. *Teachers in my school*
.. *Children in my class*

Talk about this before starting the song.

• A song which looks at numbers comparitively.

Five Children

Demonstration

Backing

Words and Music by
Eileen Diamond

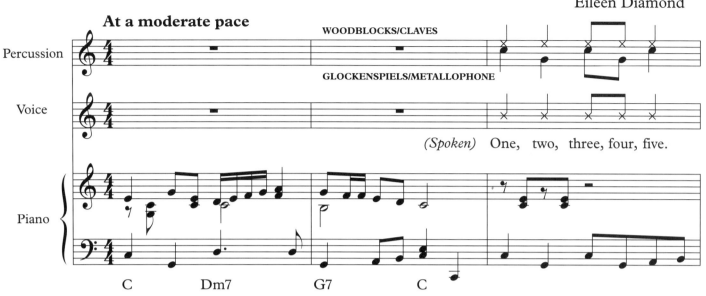

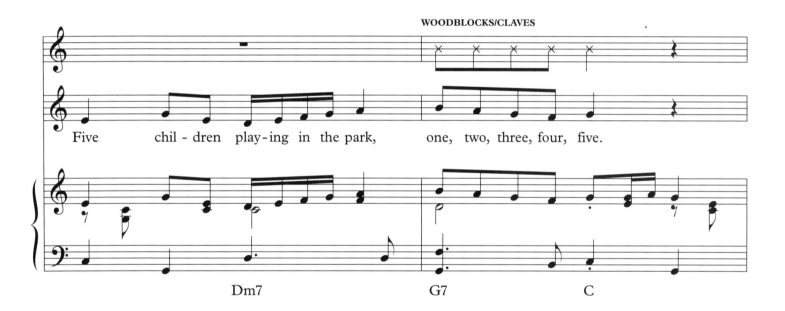

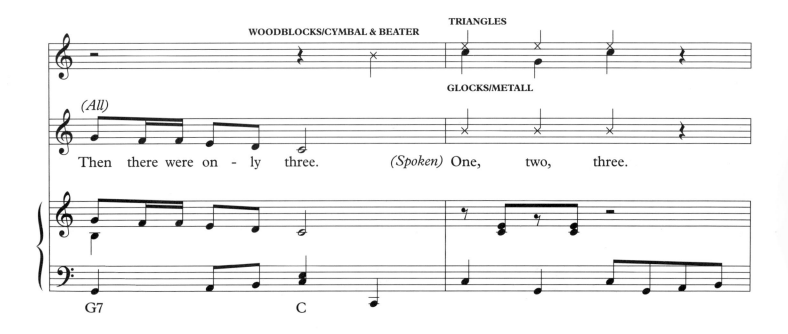

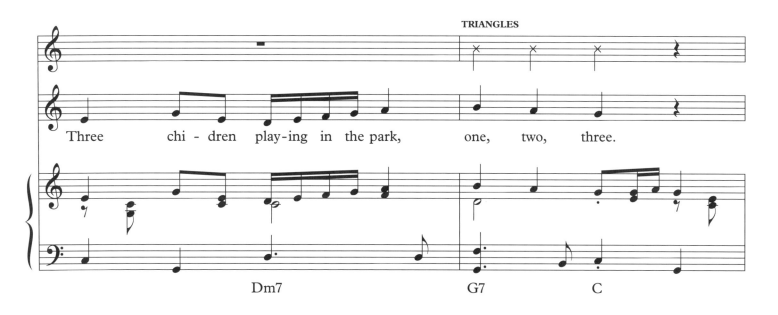

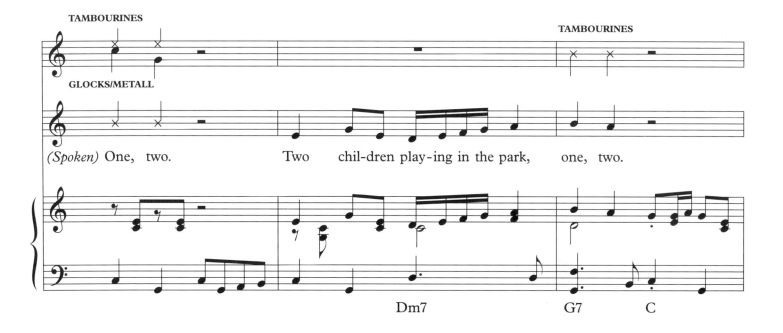

14

(4th child) One said, "I am go-ing for a run." (All) Then there was on - ly one.

Dm7   F#°   G7   C

GUIROS

A little slower

GLOCKS/METALL

(Spoken) One.   One   child   left   play-ing   in   the   park,

Dm7

GUIROS

one,   just one.   All   a - lone,   it   was-n't   a - ny   fun.

G7   C   Dm7   F#°

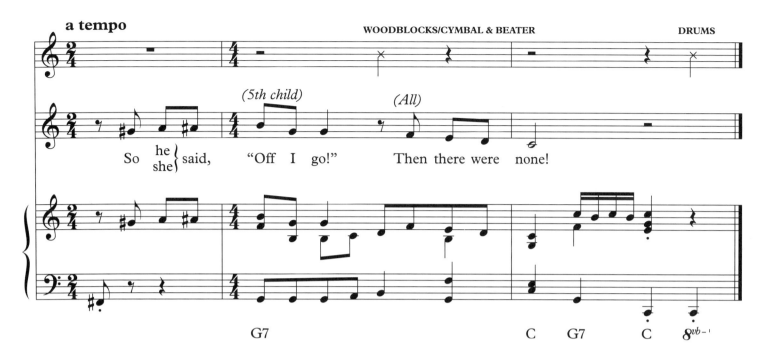

1. *One, two, three, four, five.*

   Five children playing in the park,
   One, two, three, four, five.
   One said, "I'm not playing any more."
   Then there were only four.

2. *One, two, three, four.*

   Four children playing in the park,
   One, two, three, four.
   One said, "I am going home for tea."
   Then there were only three.

3. *One, two, three.*

   Three children playing in the park,
   One, two, three.
   One said, "I have something else to do."
   Then there were only two.

4. *One, two.*

   Two children playing in the park,
   One, two.
   One said, "I am going for a run."
   Then there was only one.

5. *One.*

   One child left playing in the park,
   One, just one.
   All alone, it wasn't any fun.
   So s/he said, "Off I go!"
   Then there were none!

- Line up five children to play in the park. Teach each one their words to sing, or say if they prefer. The other children sing the song, stopping after the words *"One said"*, then coming in again with *"Then there were only..."* etc.
- The song may be performed with or without instruments.
  Any number of the following instruments may be used where indicated:
  WOODBLOCKS, CLAVES, DRUMS, TRIANGLES, TAMBOURINES, GUIROS (Scrapers),
  GLOCKENSPIELS/METALLOPHONE using notes C & G only, other bars may be removed.

Twelve Apples

Demonstration

Backing

Words and Music by
Eileen Diamond

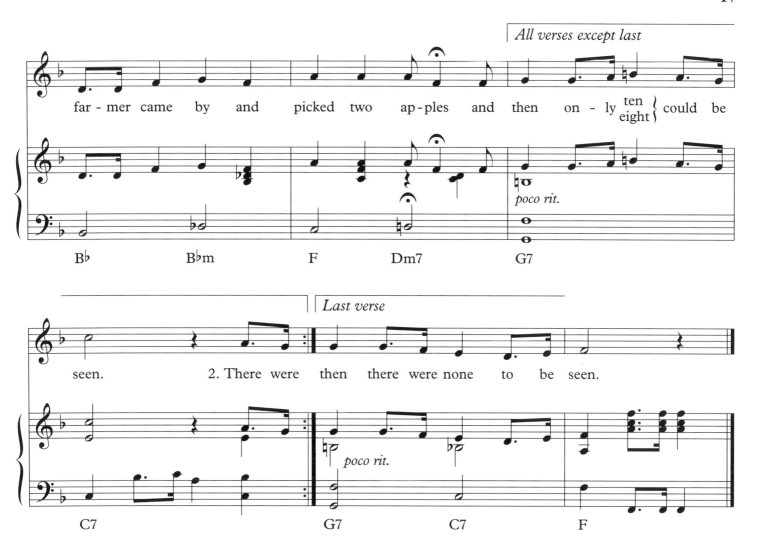

All verses except last

far - mer came by and picked two ap - ples and then on - ly ten/eight could be

B♭   B♭m   F   Dm7   G7

poco rit.

Last verse

seen.   2. There were then there were none to be seen.

poco rit.

C7   G7   C7   F

One, two, three, four, five, six, seven, eight,
Nine, ten, eleven, twelve apples.

1. There were twelve apples growing on a tree,
   Their skins were shiny and green.
   A farmer came by and picked two apples
   And then only ten could be seen.

2. There were ten apples growing on a tree,
   Their skins were shiny and green.
   A farmer came by and picked two apples
   And then only eight could be seen.

3. There were eight apples growing on a tree,
   Their skins were shiny and green.
   A farmer came by and picked two apples
   And then only six could be seen.

4. There were six apples growing on a tree,
   Their skins were shiny and green.
   A farmer came by and picked two apples
   And then only four could be seen. *(etc.)*

- A song to help with subtraction and mental arithmetic.
- Once the song is known, try changing the number of apples picked by the farmer.
- Give the children time on the pause ⌢ to work out how many apples are left.
  Percussion beats have been inserted here just to keep momentum going for the recording.
- *ACTIVITY:* A helpful prop for younger children would be a tree painted on some stiff card and put up on the wall. Then paint and cut out 12 green apples and attach them to the tree with velcro. The children can take turns acting the farmer picking the apples.

Pick A Daisy

Demonstration Backing

Words and Music by
Eileen Diamond

Not too fast, allow time for actions

more / care - ful / and / not / join / to / them / pull / care - ful-ly, / it, / then / or / the / the / chain / will / grow / long.

F♯°   C   Dm7   G7   C

2. Join the dai - sy chain will break!

poco rit.

C♯°   G   G7   Dm7   G7   C

1. Pick a daisy, pick a daisy,
   Join them up to make a chain.
   Pick another one, then another one,
   Join them up and start again.
   Pick a daisy, pick a daisy,
   Look for stems thick and strong.
   Now pick some more and join them carefully,
   Then the chain will grow long.

2. Join the first one to the last one,
   Now a circle will appear.
   Make a bracelet or a necklace,
   Or a garland you can wear.
   Count the daisies when you've finished,
   But don't make a mistake.
   Be very careful not to pull it,
   Or the daisy chain will break!

SUGGESTED ACTIONS:
- *VERSE 1:*   Choose one child to start the chain. At the words, *"Pick a daisy, pick a daisy"* s/he chooses two children and links their arms together. *"Pick another one"* etc. two more children are chosen and linked up to the first two. These actions are repeated and then *several* more children may be chosen for the last two lines.

- *VERSE 2:*   The 'Daisy Picker' joins up the chain and includes her/himself to form a circle. At the words, *"Make a bracelet"* they take a step *in* to make the circle smaller. Then one step *out* to make it bigger for a necklace and then one more step *out* to make it bigger still for a garland. They walk round while singing in the circle and fall down at the end. Tell the children to *silently* count the number of 'Daisies' in the chain and then ask one of them to say how many there are.

How Many Are There Now?

Words and Music by
Eileen Diamond

1. Three people playing together,
   Playing together, playing together.
   Now find three more people,
   How many are there now?

- A song to help counting in threes.
- Start with three people. At the words, *"Now find three more people"*, they each choose
  another player. The same children choose extra players throughout the song.
- Other numbers may also be used to help counting in twos, fours, fives, etc.
- Pause long enough after asking, *"How many are there now?"* to give children time to answer.
- Use an assortment of suitable percussion instruments and distribute them among the children.
  Choose the number of players you want to start with. They play on the beat as indicated.
  The instruments used on the recording of this song are Woodblocks and Tambourines.
- Continue the song for as long as you wish. If you want to finish at the double bar before the
  change of key, just end by playing another C chord after the pause 𝄐 .

Two Drummers

Demonstration

Backing

Words and Music by
Eileen Diamond

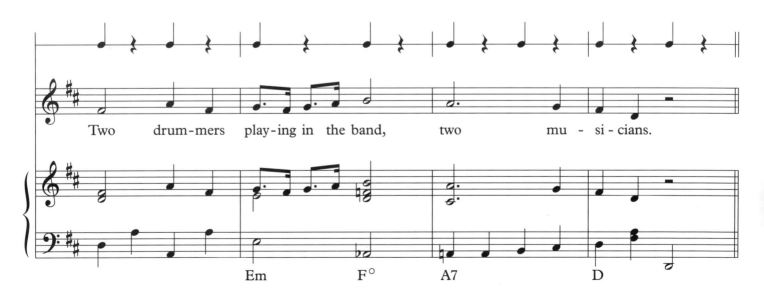

23

2. SHAKERS
3. TRIANGLES
4. WOODBLOCKS

2. Four sha - kers play - ing in the band, play - ing in the band,
3. Three trian - gles play - ing in the band, play - ing in the band,
4. Two wood-blocks play - ing in the band, play - ing in the band,

play - ing in the band. Four sha - kers play - ing in the band,
play - ing in the band. Three trian - gles play - ing in the band,
play - ing in the band. Two wood-blocks play - ing in the band,

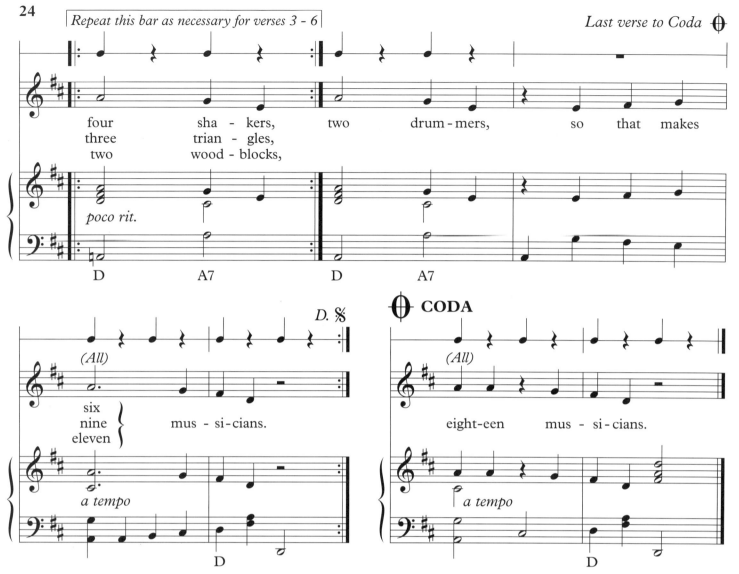

1. Two drummers playing in the band,
   Playing in the band, playing in the band.
   Two drummers playing in the band,
   TWO musicians.

2. Four shakers playing in the band,
   Playing in the band, playing in the band.
   Four shakers playing in the band,
   Four shakers, two drummers,
   So that makes SIX musicians.

3. Three triangles playing in the band,
   Playing in the band, playing in the band.
   Three triangles playing in the band,
   Three triangles, four shakers, two drummers,
   So that makes NINE musicians.

4. Two woodblocks playing in the band,
   Playing in the band, playing in the band.
   Two woodblocks playing in the band,
   Two woodblocks, three triangles,
   Four shakers, two drummers,
   So that makes ELEVEN musicians.

5. Three guiros playing in the band,
   Playing in the band, playing in the band.
   Three guiros playing in the band,
   Three guiros, two woodblocks, three triangles,
   Four shakers, two drummers,
   So that makes FOURTEEN musicians.

6. Four tambourines playing in the band,
   Playing in the band, playing in the band.
   Four tambourines, playing in the band,
   Four tambourines, three guiros, two woodblocks,
   Three triangles, four shakers, two drummers,
   So that makes EIGHTEEN musicians.

- This is an accumulative song with an extra group of instruments added at each verse.
- Select a variety of percussion instruments and choose a certain number of children to play each type of instrument. For example, see above. Use as many verses as you want.
- At the 'Repeat' bar, the instrumental groups join in one by one in accordance with the words and ALL play the last two bars together.
- Change the numbers of instruments each time the song is performed to encourage listening, concentration and mental arithmetic.

Printed and bound in Great Britain 3/01